The CQ Press Career Guide
for Public Sector Students

The CQ Press Career Guide for Public Sector Students

Michelle C. Pautz

University of Dayton

FOR INFORMATION:

CQ Press
An Imprint of SAGE Publications, Inc.
2455 Teller Road
Thousand Oaks, California 91320
E-mail: order@sagepub.com

SAGE Publications Ltd.
1 Oliver's Yard
55 City Road
London EC1Y 1SP
United Kingdom

SAGE Publications India Pvt. Ltd.
B 1/I 1 Mohan Cooperative Industrial Area
Mathura Road, New Delhi 110 044
India

SAGE Publications Asia-Pacific Pte. Ltd.
18 Cross Street #10-10/11/12
China Square Central
Singapore 048423

Acquisitions Editor: Scott Greenan
Editorial Assistant: Lauren Younker
Production Editor: Jyothi Sriram
Copy Editor: Laurie Pitman
Typesetter: Hurix Digital
Proofreader: Sarah Duffy
Cover Designer: Candice Harman
Marketing Manager: Jennifer Jones

Printed in the United States of America

Library of Congress Cataloging-in-Publication Data

Names: Pautz, Michelle C., author.

Title: The CQ Press career guide for public sector students / Michelle C. Pautz, University of Dayton.

Description: First edition. | Washington : SAGE, [2020] | Includes bibliographical references.

Identifiers: LCCN 2018044703 | ISBN 9781544345840 (saddle stitch : alk. paper)

Subjects: LCSH: Political science—Vocational guidance—United States. | College graduates—Employment—United States.

Classification: LCC JA88.U6 P38 2020 | DDC 351.73023—dc23
LC record available at https://lccn.loc.gov/2018044703

This book is printed on acid-free paper.

MIX
Paper from
responsible sources
FSC
www.fsc.org   FSC® C008955

19 20 21 22 23 10 9 8 7 6 5 4 3 2 1

CONTENTS

PREFACE

INTRODUCTION

As we look at the world around us, no matter where we identify ourselves politically or what issues we prioritize, there are changes we would all like to see in society and government. And more often than not, those changes are actioned by the individuals who work in the public sector. Over the years, as I work with undergraduate and graduate students, I find constant inspiration in those students and their desires to make the world a better place. And in conversations with these individuals, I am regularly reminded how intimidating the public sector can appear from the outside, how confusing it seems, and how hard it is to navigate those initial professional steps in public service. Accordingly, this guide captures the themes of so many of those conversations that I have with students as they sought to serve the public in a range of capacities. I offer no assurances that this guide will help you instantly figure it all out (indeed, I still have much to figure out!), but what I hope this guide will do is help you demystify the public sector, think seriously about a career in it, and engage in some activities that will help you figure it out.

I am deeply appreciative of all the students who have allowed me to walk with them during parts of their journey to finding meaningful and fulfilling work in the public sector and to chip away at the problems they see around us. These students and all the public servants motivate me and inspire me daily.

WHY I STUDY PUBLIC ADMINISTRATION AND DO WHAT I DO

Before I can offer you thoughts and activities to help you find your path, it's only fair that I share a bit of my story about how I came to be fascinated by the public sector and have devoted my professional life to education for the public sector. Growing up, I always loved social studies. And I couldn't watch or read enough news coverage as a middle and high school student. I am not sure what accounts for this fascination as my parents both vote regularly and pay attention, but they aren't captivated by the government the way I am.

When I started my college career, I wanted to major in film studies because I loved movies and worked in movie theaters and video stores. But I didn't want to make movies, I just wanted to study them and evaluate them. I was unsure how this would offer me a future after school. My other passion was government but I had no idea what I would do after college with government, but I knew I needed to get a job. I didn't think I could get a job with a degree in political science—little did I know—so I majored in economics thinking that still involved the government but was in the business school, so I must be able to get a job. While I was in college, I realized I could add both political science and public administration as majors and still graduate on time, so I did. And I came to understand the range of job possibilities in these fields.

I took a course in environmental policy in my sophomore year that I loved. I'm not quite sure why it resonated with me—I remember how great and motivating the professor was, but I wasn't particularly enamored with environmentalism prior to the course. The next semester I took an environmental economics course and was equally inspired. As luck would have it, one of my professors told me about a state government internship program. So, I checked it out. I had no idea what an internship was really all about, but I knew it was better that I do something like that rather than work in a movie theater for yet another summer. Ultimately, I interned for what was then called the North Carolina Department of Environment and Natural Resources, and I was hooked. I was fascinated by environmental regulations, the workings of government, and how stuff got done. I continued interning there for another summer.

My undergraduate theses looked at different aspects of environmental policy, and I wanted to learn more. Since I was little, I always wanted to teach, but I didn't think that I wanted to teach elementary or high school. By the end of my college career, another professor of mine suggested I consider graduate school in public administration and that sounded like a great idea—if I'm being honest, I mostly wanted to delay any adult decision making for another couple of years, so a master's degree seemed perfect. In the back of my mind, I thought that if I could make it in graduate school, maybe I would get a PhD and become a college professor. The rest, as they say, is history.

ACKNOWLEDGMENTS

My journey owes much to a number of individuals along the way that talked with me and helped me figure out what I was passionate about and what I wanted to pursue professionally. Dr. Sharon Spray and Dr. Doug Redington, both of Elon University, were undergraduate professors of mine that shaped my interests in environmental issues. Dr. Chalmers Brumbaugh and Dr. Betty Morgan have both retired from Elon, but were instrumental in helping me pursue those first internship experiences and find my way to Virginia Tech. In graduate school, Dr. Karen Hult and Dr. Larkin Dudley played major roles in helping me refine my passions, as did my fellow graduate students. Then as a professor, I continue to encounter students who inspire and motivate me—including a number of them profiled in the following pages.

But I would be remiss if I didn't acknowledge my family. My husband, Steven, is a dedicated federal civil servant himself. And I'm inspired by and incredibly proud of the work he does. It's not easy being a civil servant and he's dedicated himself to public service. And it's not easy being married to someone like me who studies the public sector and always has bizarre questions or abstract theories to contextualize what he might be experiencing in his day-to-day work. It takes a special kind of person to put up with that. Beyond his professional pursuits, he provides unwavering and unconditional support for my professional aspirations. The love he offers is enhanced by the affection and attention of our three amazing dogs, Sydney, Victoria, and Mackenzie. Their support is of a far different nature, but their wagging tails, understanding looks, and general presence are essential in keeping me grounded and motivating me.

ABOUT THE AUTHOR

 **Michelle C. Pautz** is an associate professor of political science and assistant provost for the Common Academic Program at the University of Dayton. Her research has appeared in *Administration & Society*, *Administrative Theory & Praxis*, *Journal of Political Science Education*, *Journal of Environmental Studies & Sciences*, *Journal of Public Affairs Education*, *Policy Studies Journal*, *PS: Political Science & Politics*, *Public Voices*, and the *Review of Policy Research*, among others. She is the author of *Civil Servants on the Silver Screen: Hollywood's Depiction of Government and Bureaucrats*; coauthor of *Public Policy: A Concise Introduction*, *The Lilliputians of Environmental Regulation: The Perspective of State Regulators*, and *U.S. Environmental Policy in Action: Practice and Implementation*; and coeditor of *The Intersection of Food and Public Health: Current Policy Challenges and Solutions*. She holds a PhD in public administration and an MPA from Virginia Tech. She earned a BA in economics, political science, and public administration from Elon University.

CHAPTER ONE

DEFINING THE PUBLIC SECTOR AND ITS OPPORTUNITIES

Undoubtedly, you have heard the term the *public sector*, but you may not have a clear sense of what that term implies, let alone the career possibilities it holds. Don't worry, you're not alone. By contrast, the *private sector* often seems much clearer as it refers to the companies that make the stuff we buy, like cell phones, or that provide the services we consume, like movie-streaming services. And these private sector companies make huge profits, or at least strive to do that. But what is it that the public sector actually does, and what kinds of meaningful career opportunities does it offer? These questions are the foundation of this chapter, so we will

- define the public sector,

- discuss the range of career options available in the public sector, and

- explore public perceptions and attitudes about the public sector and the people who work in it.

This last objective is particularly important because there are a lot of perceptions about the public sector that would likely impact anyone's consideration of a career; therefore, it is essential to acknowledge and understand those attitudes and where they come from. By the end of this chapter, you should have a good understanding of the public sector and the wide variety of job opportunities you could pursue.

WHAT IS THE PUBLIC SECTOR?

The *public sector* is a term that refers to the organizations that provide public goods and services, ranging from the military and law enforcement, to roads and bridges, to environmental protection and food safety. These are goods and services that are intended for the general public, not necessarily for any one person's individual welfare. You may be looking at this book as part of a public policy or a public administration course and many of the topics in that course are in the purview of the public sector. The organizations engaged in these activities might be government entities or non profit organizations. These organizations might be federal, state, or local government agencies; they might be a huge non profit organization that has locations all over the country, or perhaps even the world; or they might be a small non profit organization serving the needs of your community. Public sector organizations are as varied and diverse as their private sector counterparts.

Perhaps you are interested in environmental issues and sustainability, so let's think about the range of public sector organizations whose missions are focused in that area. In terms of government agencies, there is the U.S. Environmental Protection Agency based in Washington, D.C., and has field offices all over the United States, then each state has a state-level environmental agency (as does the District of Columbia), such as the Ohio Environmental Protection Agency. The vast majority of those state agencies have a centralized headquarters location, as well as field offices throughout the state. Then in some states, there are local or regional government agencies that work on environmental issues, too, such as the Regional Air Pollution Control Agency (RAPCA), based in Dayton, Ohio, or the Miami Conservancy District, also in Dayton. If you're keeping a tally, there's already a lot of government agencies involved, but that doesn't account for the non profit organizations, including the Sierra Club or the Ocean Conservancy, which are major, national organizations (and many have local or regional chapters or offices) and smaller, more narrowly focused organizations, such as Appalachian Voices or the Chesapeake Climate Action Network. The point is that within even one specific policy area, the number of public organizations involved in efforts to improve the health of the environment and promote sustainability number in the hundreds, if not thousands, of organizations that have people who work for them to carry out their missions.

The missions and the tasks of organizations in the public sector are quite a bit different than those of private sector organizations. Just think about the example organizations already mentioned in this chapter. Apple makes a range of consumer electronics, from iPhones to Apple Watches, and there are many movie-streaming services, from Amazon Prime to Netflix, that afford us the opportunity to watch movies at any time on our own electronic devices. Now, think about the U.S. Environmental Protection Agency. Its mission is to protect human health and the environment. The Chesapeake Climate Action Network is a regional organization based in Maryland that strives to fight climate change. The Federal Aviation Administration is essential in managing the airspace above us for planes to take us from one place to another.

Public and private sector organizations vary in what they do. The work involved in developing the iPhone, in terms of both the physical construction as well as the software that makes it indispensable to many of us, undoubtedly took lots of time, money, and ingenuity, but the tasks before private sector organizations are very different than those of public sector organizations. Government and non profit organizations strive to serve the public by advancing efforts around reducing environmental harms or making sure that the planes do not collide midair. It is reasonable to stipulate that these are very different kinds of organizational tasks.

Although there are many similarities between public and private organizations, as they are comprised of people trying to achieve certain goals and objectives, the differences between them are far more significant. As we have already seen, the missions of public organizations are far different from those of private organizations first and foremost. Second, authority structures also differ. In the case of Apple, where does it derive power and authority? From Apple stockholders and its customers. Apple can charge $1,000 for its iPhone X because its customers are willing to pay for it (and line up at all hours of the day to be one of the first proud new owners of the device!), and people clamor to buy Apple stock. And these forces help keep Tim Cook as the company's chief executive officer. What about the United States Postal Service (USPS)? The head of the USPS is the postmaster general (the first of whom was Benjamin Franklin) and is appointed by the Board of Governors of the USPS (akin to a board of directors), but those governors are appointed by the president and confirmed by the Senate. At best, the USPS customers have an indirect effect on the agency's leadership. The USPS relies on Congress for its budget. To increase the cost of mailing a letter, the USPS has to navigate the administrative process to propose and approve a rate increase. And while the USPS is a rarity in that it has private sector counterparts (think UPS or FedEx), most government agencies do not have competition (after all, what other organization controls air traffic?). But the USPS is required, by law, to serve every address in the United States, something none of its competitors do (there are many rural addresses that private sector companies won't serve because it is not cost-effective for them to do so).

Third, the work of public organizations, such as the USPS, also exists in a broader political landscape, complete with sensitivity to the next election cycle and what changes in party control might mean for the organization. Politicians play a role in the senior leadership of these organizations as well as appropriating funds for the organizations to pursue their missions. Non profit organizations are also sensitive to politics since many organizations rely on government grants to carry out some of the work, or may partner with government agencies to provide services for citizens. And finally, public organizations are far more likely to be involved in the lives of citizens, whether citizens like it or not. After all, if you are not a fan of the iPhone or the Apple OS, then you would probably buy an Android phone, and avoid all things Apple. Whether you realize it or not, the USPS is instrumental in your life, along with many other public organizations. You may not even realize the work the Ocean Conservancy does to educate people and the food service industry about sustainable fishing practices when you eat fish tacos, for example. So, given the differences in tasks, authority, political context, and involvement in daily lives, the work of public organizations varies quite a bit from private sector organizations.

Application Activity

With this understanding of the public sector and the range of organizations that comprise it, you are now in a position to think about the kinds of public organizations you might be interested in. In the first activity designed to help you figure out if the public sector may be right for you, make a list of three areas of activity that the public sector engages in that you find interesting. For example, these might be growing concerns over food deserts, particularly in urban areas, or local government efforts to promote sustainability, or programs to provide young people with after-school support. Then, do some Internet searching and find a few specific organizations near you that engage in these kinds of activities. Have a look at these organizations' websites and get a sense of their size, their mission, and their efforts. You may very well be surprised about the scope of these organizations' work!

PERCEPTIONS AND MYTHS ABOUT THE PUBLIC SECTOR

Now that you have given some thought to the various types of public sector organizations and the range of activities they engage in, you might find some of these entities potentially appealing to you professionally. But, if you're like most people, there is a nagging voice in the back of your head saying, sure, these may be great missions, but who wants to work in the public sector. After all, if you were to stop people outside your favorite coffee or sandwich shop and ask them what their perceptions about the public sector were, you would probably get responses like "it's full of lazy and incompetent people," or "people who can get a real job do, and those who can't work for the government," or "it's full of waste, fraud, and abuse," or "the employees are overpaid and get cushy benefits and job security." These myths about government, and even the non profit sector, are pervasive. Indeed, Americans have a love-hate relationship with government and the public sector. On the one hand, we expect much of the government, from mail delivery to airport safety to educating young people. But, on the other hand, we loathe government involvement in our lives, we don't want to be inconvenienced, and we definitely don't want to pay more in taxes than is absolutely necessary.

These conflicted attitudes are nothing new. American history reminds us how much colonists and the nation's first citizens distrusted the British monarchy, and we know what colonists thought of taxes. While disdain for the public sector is commonplace in the United States, there have been fluctuations over time. Believe it or not, there was a time in America's history when working in the public sector was thought of as noble and prestigious—something parents wanted for their sons (this was during the early years of the nation, and it was typically only men who worked outside of their home).

But since the latter part of the 20th century through today, we see downward trends in Americans' attitudes about government (with the notable exception of the aftermath of the terrorist attacks of September 11). Public trust in the federal government continues to hover at near all-time lows, with only 18 percent of Americans saying they can trust government to do what is right (Pew Research Center 2017). These negative attitudes about the public sector might help explain that while 94 percent of millennials want to use their skills to be of service and benefit a social cause, only 7 percent of the federal government workforce is under the age of 30 (Curry 2017).

Application Activity

For our next Application Activity, take a minute and write down your views and perceptions of the public sector. Are your perceptions positive or negative? Next, are you intrigued by the possibility of working in the public sector? Why or why not? Write down your responses. Third, review your perceptions about the public sector. Where do you think these attitudes came from? Were they informed by your friends and family? Direct experiences with the public sector? The news media? Be honest with yourself; you may not even be able to pinpoint where these attitudes come from—most of us probably cannot (your author included!). Now, hold on to these reflections as we explore the origins of these perceptions and attitudes.

PUBLIC SECTOR MISCONCEPTIONS

It may seem that unpacking public sector misconceptions may not be as productive as telling you how to get an internship or mapping out career paths for you. Don't worry, we will get to those topics. But before we do, we have to think about the reasons we may be skeptical of the public sector and why those people who are important in our lives may be even more concerned. In the spirit of honesty, it is important to note that most of us actually have positive experiences with the public sector even though we hold the entire sector with little regard (c.f. Charles Goodsell). After all, when was the last time you put something in the mail and worried about it getting to its destination? Or have you ever been concerned that when the trash is put on the curb that it wasn't going to be picked up by your local municipality?

The first misconception that we have to confront in understanding Americans' views of the public sector is that most of us fail to differentiate between politicians and civil servants. And since we generally don't distinguish between them, our disdain for one effects our views of the other. Politicians are those individuals who are elected to hold governmental office, such as the president, members of Congress, governors, state legislators, mayors, county commissioners, and so forth. They get their jobs from the voters, and they have to win elections to keep their jobs. Civil servants, on the other hand, are the unelected individuals who work for government agencies or non profit organizations who carry out the decisions of our elected leaders. They are the ones who provide us public goods and services. These individuals get and retain their jobs because they have demonstrated competence in the area they work in. For example, many of the individuals who work in environmental agencies have training and degrees in environmental and earth sciences, engineering, or even environmental economics. By contrast, members of Congress write environmental legislation and many—or most—do not have this kind of training. Many members have law degrees.

The numbers of the civil servant workforce might astound you. In the United States, there is the federal government, 50 state governments, and just over 89,000 local governments (U.S. Census Bureau 2012). That's a lot of government entities! According to the U.S. Office of Personnel Management (OPM), there are 2.8 million federal government civil servants, and this figure does not include members of the military. In state and local government agencies, there are another 14.5 million civil servants (U.S. Census Bureau 2016). In the more than 1.4 million non profit organizations in the United States, there are approximately 14.4 million employees (McKeever and Gaddy 2016). With these numbers, you are far more likely to know, and even have family members who are, civil servants than you are to know a politician.

The distinction between politicians and civil servants is important to understanding our perceptions because most Americans do not like (and that's probably putting it mildly) politicians. So when we think about government, our attitudes about politicians are usually what we think of rather than separating views of politicians from views of civil servants. Pollsters will routinely ask Americans about their views of Democrats and Republicans and the leadership of various elected bodies. And the queries are typically around government broadly, reinforcing the collapsing of the two categories.

Another misconception might be that the people who are civil servants are lazy or incompetent or corrupt. Again, a part of this myth is the conflating of politicians and civil servants—but this is not the place to unpack the realities of elected leaders as we are focused on the rest of the public sector. Who really are civil servants? As indicated above, chances are good that you know some. In my own family, there is a civil servant who works for the U.S. Department of Defense, a public school teacher, a local government sanitation employee, and a USPS employee. Other civil servants I know well range from local government employees, to law enforcement officers, to first responders. And without a doubt, all of these people I know are competent and committed individuals who have chosen careers in the public sector over the private sector because they want to be of service, not because they are looking for a cushy, well-paying job. Despite popular opinion, most government salaries lag behind those of private sector employees (Yoder 2018). And unlike the demographics of politicians, the demographics of civil servants look more like the average American (Goodsell 2015, 81-119). According to the OPM, 57 percent of federal civil servants are men, 43 percent are women. About 37 percent of them identify with a minority ethnic group and 52 percent of them hold a bachelor's degree or higher (U.S. OPM 2017).

After confronting misconceptions about the public sector and those individuals who work in it, we also need to investigate what our actual experiences with the public sector are and separate out our views of politics and politicians. Charles Goodsell (2015) began unpacking questions about the attitudes we have about government and comparing them to our actual experiences decades ago. In his most recent updates to this research in *The New Case for Bureaucracy*, he found that despite holding negative views of government, most Americans have positive interactions and experiences with government (41-77). Relying on data from a variety of surveys and interviews with individuals, Goodsell concludes that the actual experiences we have with the public sector are overwhelmingly positive, from the local parks we visit to the snowplowing in the winter to garbage collection and mail delivery.

In light of these discussions, you are probably wondering why there is such a disconnect between our perceptions of the public sector and our actual experiences with it. Political socialization provides a substantial part of the answer to this question. As you might remember, political socialization is the process by which we come to have the beliefs we do about government and its role in society. We are not born with these views or attitudes, rather we learn them over time. Various influences contribute to our socialization, including our family and friends, education, personal experiences, religious affiliations, news media, and popular culture. Consider this last influence: popular culture. Our history as a nation reveals a deep disdain for centralized authority and government; just think about our origin stories associated with breaking free of the tyrannical British government and the colonists' rebellion over taxes. We have been distrustful of government from the beginning. And now, think about popular music, television programs, and even movies. Can you think of any movies or television shows in which the government is portrayed particularly well? Do you know of any musicians who write songs about how great it is to put a present in the mail to someone and not worry about it getting there?

Let's explore one aspect of popular culture a bit more to illustrate more deeply one of the various influences on political socialization. In the movies, government broadly is portrayed negatively (Pautz 2018). The 2016 Disney film *Zootopia* is about a city of anthropomorphic animals in which a rookie bunny cop and a con artist fox have to work together to uncover a conspiracy. And in the movie, there is a bureau of motor vehicles agent that is literally played by a sloth. One would be hard pressed to be any clearer about sending a message about civil servants who work in the BMV than a literal sloth portraying the character. By contrast, when renewing my driver's license recently, I went to my local motor vehicles office that had a pleasant enough waiting area where no one had to stand in line since we all took a number and could have a seat wherever we wanted while we waited. When it was my turn, the clerk was more than efficient, and was slowed down only while waiting for me to pay my renewal fee. In all honesty, I have probably waited longer for my coffee at my local Starbucks. Movies matter in their portrayals of government and their potential effects on our political socialization for a number of reasons. First, when we watch movies, we're typically doing it to be entertained (unless you're in my film and politics course!), so we let our guard down and we aren't critically evaluating the images we see. This leaves us open to influence. Second, watching movies, particularly in the cinema, immerses our senses. It is one of the few times that the distractions of our small screens are set aside while we watch a big screen. This is potentially very powerful in its ability to influence us. Additionally, young people—those under 25— are the most likely to watch movies, and they are in their most formative years for their political socialization. In other words, the images that young people see may be even more powerful and influential.

All of these influences that are a part of our political socialization are neither good nor bad; they are simply influences. They are discussed here because understanding them helps us figure out where our attitudes about government— and more importantly for our purposes—the public sector come from. Just as it is essential to think about civil servants as distinct from politicians when we talk about government, it is important to understand our attitudes about government and their origins when we consider pursuing a career in the public sector as they may be influencing whether or not we think the public sector might be a meaningful and viable career path. If we understand how we perceive the public sector, we may be able to separate our views based on experiences and our views based on other influences and this may open us to the possibilities in the public sector.

Application Activity

The Application Activity at the end of the last section asked you to identify your attitudes and perceptions of the public sector. In the final activity for this chapter, go back to your notes from that effort, and in light of what you have learned in this section, let's see if we can pinpoint some of their origins. Write down the most recent experiences you had with the public sector. Were those experiences mailing a package at the Post Office? Interacting with a law enforcement officer? Attending a local government meeting? Now think about some of the images of the public sector we are bombarded with in our culture; make a list of three examples of incompetence in the public sector from entertainment or news media. Now make a list of three examples of competence in the public sector from the media. Which list was easier to come up with? Why do you think that list was easier than the other? This exercise will help further your understanding of your political socialization and the influences that are particularly strong. Doing so might enable you to think about a public sector career in a new light and remove (or at least push to the side) common perceptions about the ineptitude of the public sector to allow you to see the possibilities.

CHAPTER WRAP-UP

Exploring a career path in the public sector requires us to understand the public sector, what it entails, and to confront some perceptions about it. In this chapter, we have discussed the vastness of the public sector in the United States, delineated the work of civil servants from the work of politicians, and considered where some of the erroneous perceptions we often have about the public sector come from. This establishes the foundation upon which we can discuss strategies for figuring out if a public sector career path is right for you. In the next chapter, we explore how your college courses can help you further this investigation.

ACTION ITEMS

After reading this chapter, you should have (1) identified some areas of public sector activities that interest you and (2) considered your own views and perceptions of the public sector and where those beliefs might have come from. With these interests articulated, find three public sector organizations that are interesting to you. Look at their websites and social media presence. For each of the three, identify the mission of the organization, explore the backgrounds and job descriptions of the people who work there, and find out from their website or by getting in touch with their human resources department or contact if they offer internship positions and what the requirements are for those positions.

PUBLIC SECTOR PROFILE

Robin J. Bachman, Chief, Policy Coordination Office, and Chief Privacy Officer, U.S. Census Bureau, U.S. Department of Commerce[1]

Robin J. Bachman earned a Bachelor of Arts degree from Miami University in political science and American studies and went on to earn a Master of Public Administration degree from Virginia Tech. She works for the U.S. Census Bureau in Washington, D.C.

1. **What is your current job and how did your studies prepare you for this role? How does that job align with what you thought you'd be doing when you were in college?**

---

[1] Disclaimer: The replies to these questions are Ms. Bachman's own and do not necessarily represent the views of her agency. She contributed to this Q and A in her personal capacity.

I have fond memories of my undergrad studies. I am a Miami University alumna. My college years helped me pick my path. I started school in the business program and after a few classes realized that I needed to keep exploring other fields of study because I would be a truly unhappy accountant. Because of the strong liberal arts offerings at Miami of Ohio, I was able to find a better fit for me, government and non profit work.

My job aligns very well with my major and graduate work. However, the question made me smile: I envy those who can image long time horizons; after I realized I did not want to be an accountant, I took all four years of school to figure out what job I might be able to land upon completion of my undergraduate degree. And with the economy in recession when I graduated, I felt very fortunate when I was hired three months after graduation.

2. What were some of the classes that really stood out to you in school that were influential in finding your career path?

My undergraduate classes that were smaller, discussion-based, encouraged critical thinking, and included a strong writing component are the more memorable ones for me. For instance, Women in Politics was an important class because it introduced me to national leaders that I did not know and opened my eyes to the work of America's women trailblazers. I took a First Amendment and Free Speech class that taught me about the courts and how to dig into case law. My American Studies courses were some of my favorite because of their interdisciplinary approach to subjects. In grad school, one of my best classes was Normative Foundations. I also valued being able to enhance my educational experience by taking classes in other departments. To this day I still quote performance = motivation x ability from my Industrial and Organizational Psychology class, and from Communication's Public Relations Theory and Practice, I often probe at work if we are establishing a two-way symmetrical relationship with our audiences. I attended graduate school 11 years after I graduated with my bachelor's; pursuing my master's was a time to reflect and spend focused energy on my studies. I appreciated the professors that helped me hone my writing and challenged me with weighty topics, including those beyond the practical day-to-day application of the public sector craft. Graduate school was a place I explored the nexus between non profits and government and how they collectively advance the common good.

3. What are some classes you wish you took now that you didn't take or didn't have the chance to take in college?

There is never enough time to take all the classes one wants to take, but in my current post I am reminded that even more grounding in these areas would help me manage my office and my 38+ staff, classes like applied public sector budgeting, finance, appropriations law; acquisitions and contracting; and personnel/human resources management. And because I am at a statistical agency, there are some days I wish I would have kept going in statistics and research methodology. The good news is there is lifelong learning; the federal government offers training, too.

4. What internships and/or co-curricular activities did you participate in and how did they prepare you for your graduate work and/or professional trajectory?

During my undergraduate years, I was very active in organizations, particularly College Democrats. It was the relationships I developed during these co-curricular moments that helped me figure out my career/life path and gain my first job. They were also a saving grace, for when I was struggling to figure out my academic self, my activities made sense. It took me a minute, but I finally figured out that there was an academic connection to the campaign work we were doing in our after-class organizations and school: I could major in political science. I ended up running for local city council my senior year, too (a story for another time). Additionally, I was in the Honors Program; it had a focus on studies but also had a tight-knit social component. Some of my best friends to this day are friends I met in the Honors Program. It also led me to a summer internship in Hamilton, Ohio, with the Hamilton Appalachian Peoples Service Organization (HAPSO). HAPSO introduced me to the Ohio Appalachian community, its history and its people. HAPSO also gave me a first hand look at the importance of good governance and how non profits struggle without solid financial footing.

In grad school, I became a graduate assistant in the Institute for Governance and Accountabilities, School of Public and International Affairs. I helped create and implement the Leadership through the Arts Program, an effort to revitalize Virginia's Dan River Region. It was a good application of my MPA studies and my earlier government experience. I also really enjoyed that our research took us to Southside Virginia and we engaged with persons beyond the classroom.

5. What advice would you give to your undergraduate self? Or, in other words, what do you wish you knew as an undergraduate that you know now?

When I was trying to figure out my major, I wish I would have sought more counsel, including talking to an academic advisor. I do not recall seeking out advice and, to be honest, it was a lonely moment during my sophomore year. I am the first in my immediate family to go to school; therefore, I did not have family to turn to for guidance. I remember at one point in my sophomore year when I realized I wanted to leave the business program, I considered dropping out because I was not sure what one did when "the plan" was no longer a good one. Luckily, I had started my American studies classes the same time I started my business ones, and realized that the arts and sciences were the better path. My advice would be to ask for help if you need it. It is a lesson I believe I have learned. Relatedly, I would recommend talking out some of your decisions. That same year, I was enrolled in a public speaking communications class. It was a requirement for business majors and very hard to get into. I dropped the class when I made the decision to move to political science and American studies. But taking a step back, it is and was a very helpful class no matter what one's discipline, but I dropped it to completely pivot to my new major. I still shake my head at that decision. The last bit of advice I would offer would be to enjoy your classes, all of them. Life, including one's professional life, is a tapestry of many interconnected topics; knowledge and learning enrich the whole experience.

CHAPTER TWO

CURRICULUM CONSIDERATIONS

Simply understanding what the public sector encompasses is a huge step in thinking about potential career paths. In this chapter, we focus on the academic side of your college experience to think through what courses, programs, and opportunities might enable you to contemplate a public sector career while pursuing your degree. More specifically, in this chapter we will

- investigate which academic programs, majors, and minors might be a good fit for your interests and professional goals;

- discuss how to maximize the opportunities every class you have to take—yes, even those required general education courses—can help you figure out your path in the public sector; and

- explain how your coursework can be of particular interest to prospective employers and discuss how to pull together effectively your academic experiences in portfolios and for job interviews.

It can often be challenging to think about how the professional aspirations you have may be pursued in the day-to-day routine of your college educational experience. Believe it or not, so much of college can and does feed into your professional path. But this is not to stress you out, leading you to believe that you have to figure out and make the right decisions, right now. Most of us who are years into our professional careers will readily admit how winding our paths have really been.

SELECTING ACADEMIC PROGRAMS, MAJORS, AND MINORS

It is completely understandable that after reading the first chapter, you might think that you have to major in political science, or some closely related field (such as government or public policy), to pursue a career in the public sector. This could not be further from the truth. Quite honestly, any academic program would prepare you for a public sector career. Engineers are regularly hired by the government; they find jobs in transportation departments and consumer product safety organizations. Scientists work for the Department of Defense, the U.S. Geological Survey, the Food and Drug Administration, the Department of Health and Human Services, not to mention lots of state and local government agencies. Accountants and financial analysts find jobs in *every* public sector organization, government and non profit. Even individuals with education degrees do not just work as teachers or administrators in America's schools; they work for departments of education, after-school or enrichment program organizations, and even policy research entities. All of this is said to help calm nerves when it comes to selecting a major.

In my own journey, I remember how daunting it seemed to be to select a major, and I regularly see the same struggle in the students I work with, including graduate students. It is completely normal to be overwhelmed with these choices as they seem extremely consequential as they appear to dictate the rest of your life. The first thing to remember in selecting a major or academic program is that you do not have to fret about finding *the* perfect major or program. This doesn't mean that you should select a major by throwing a dart at the board and pursuing a major based on where the dart lands, but it does mean that your choice of major does not and will not define your professional life, unless of course you want it to. The world is full of people who majored in something in college that is unrelated to what they do now. I know education majors who work for intelligence agencies, English majors who work for a public health department, and philosophy majors who work as lobbyists, just as a few examples. Be thoughtful about your decisions as to what to study in college, but keep in mind that those decisions do not have to dictate the rest of your career—college is just the beginning.

Once you've taken a few deep breaths and realized that your major selection doesn't have to be perfect, it's important to be honest with yourself about what you do and do not want to study in college. So, often students talk with me about the struggle between selecting a major that they think is a good major and will lead to a good job (and perhaps influenced by the desires of other people in the student's life) and the major or area of study that is interesting and exciting to them. In these conversations, honesty is essential. First, what makes for a good job in your view? How do you define *good*? Then, think about your own interests. What are you interested in? Why are you interested in it? What motivates you? What gets you excited about it? If you start with your own interests and passions and let those drive your decision making around academic programs, I guarantee you that you will be happier and more likely to find a meaningful professional path than if you let other people or other factors drive those choices. After all, we are talking about academic decisions that are about *your* education and *your* professional life, not the lives and paths of others. Every day of the semester, you're the one who has to take those classes, complete those assignments, and graduate. You should study what you're interested in.

While the discussion so far has hopefully alleviated some pressure, it still doesn't provide you the answers to how to select the major, minors, or programs that are right for you. The single biggest piece of advice is to talk to people, lots of people. Engage in conversation—and probably multiple conversations—with people who know you (or get to know you) and people that you respect. And you need to talk to more than one person because everyone has their own point of view and their own dispositions. For example, I am someone who thought a lot about going to law school but I ultimately chose graduate school instead. When students come to me, weighing the pros and cons of law school, I have opinions that are shaped by my own decisions not to go to law school, and while I believe I can talk with them about these decisions, I know I have my own biases. So, I tell them that and I urge them to go talk to other people and get other points of view. I don't want to say this is never the case, but usually more information is a good thing when making a decision.

So, who should you talk to? You should talk with your academic advisor, faculty members, fellow students, friends, alumni and staff in your college's career center, people you meet in various activities, and even people who work in areas that you think you might have a professional interest in. Ask these individuals about programs and majors; ask them about their paths and how they figured out what to major in.

Besides talking to people, you should also use your college career as an opportunity to try things out. As many parents are fond of saying, how do you know you don't like broccoli unless you've tried it? The same can be said for academic programs. If you are intrigued by a subject, take a class or two in it; who knows, you may find you love accounting. Or, if you take a few economics courses, you might discover you absolutely hate it—better to find out a few classes in to a major rather than when you graduate and receive your degree in that subject! We'll delve more into course selection in the next section.

Application Activity

Now that we have discussed that there is no perfect major to select to pursue a career in the public sector, we are ready for our first Application Activity of the chapter. First, open up a blank document or get out a piece of paper. Number it 1 to 10. Then, set a timer for three minutes. In those three minutes, write down 10 things that motivate you, that interest you. With this list, now peruse your college or university's website and look at the academic programs it offers. Start by just taking in the list of options. I continue to be impressed by all the programs that students can select from. Then, look at the list of 10 things that interest you and motivate you. See where there might be intersection between the 10 and the programs at your institution. Identify the programs that seem interesting to you. Do some digging; read the descriptions of these programs. Look at the lists of courses that comprise the major or minor. See what recent graduates of those programs are doing now. If you can't find enough information online or want more information, reach out to those departments or programs and ask to talk to someone. I can assure you that department chairs and faculty members in those programs are excited by their programs and would love to talk with you—indeed, talking with you about why what they do is awesome is way more interesting than some of the mundane work that their job entails!

PICKING COURSES

Selecting a major (and any minors) helps guide course selection—after all, to earn a degree in that particular area, there is certain content that faculty members and academic institutions have determined to be essential to that area. And within those majors, there is often some flexibility or options for you to pick which courses you want to take. But majors and minors don't account for all the courses that you take as part of your college education—there are also general education courses. In this section, we're going to examine the course options you do have, regardless of major, and discuss different kinds of courses that might be advantageous to you in a public sector career. First, we'll reflect on general education curriculum and its purpose, and then we'll consider what are some overarching topics and kinds of courses that you should think about taking.

For many students, general education courses can seem pointless. After all, if you are majoring in economics, why should you take history courses? If you are studying English, why do you need to take natural science courses? While these questions are commonplace, they neglect the rationale of general education requirements. In most colleges and universities, earning a degree in a particular field requires course-work outside of one's major. This coursework can look very different from institution to institution, but there are two points to note. First, these additional curricular requirements were arrived at intentionally by the faculty and administration of your institution. Broadly speaking, general education requirements are designed to give you the knowledge and skills that all individuals with a college education should have, regardless of major. General education curricula often emphasize critical thinking, analytical skills development, and written and oral communication, among others, that are essential professionally.

Additionally, many institutions require coursework in humanities, social sciences, natural sciences, and the visual and performing arts. Taking courses in these areas, especially if they are outside your field of study, helps you understand how other fields (and the people trained in these areas) approach issues and solve problems. Understanding different ways of thinking and understanding different ways of addressing challenges are invaluable. Very rarely in your professional life will you approach a challenge and say, "Wait a minute, we should only look at this problem from one point of view." The challenges in the workplace (and arguably in life, too) rarely, if ever, respect the nice, neat disciplinary boundaries that our fields or majors would have us believe exist. The issues we face transcend those disciplinary boundaries, and we have to have a background in lots of areas to address those issues. It is unfortunate that too many students (and even a few faculty members) look at these courses outside of one's major as wasting space in your semester schedule. You should value these opportunities to learn about different approaches to issues, to meet and interact with people from other areas of study, and to prepare yourself for a lifetime of tackling challenges from multiple points of view.

Use this mindset when you are approaching course selections, both inside and outside of your major. Your future employers want you to have a well-rounded education and not just be extremely well trained in environmental science, for example. Breadth of knowledge is just as important as depth in one's major.

As you consider a public sector career, there are various areas of coursework that could prove beneficial:

- **Government and politics courses,** such as American politics and government, state and local government, and related courses, might be advantageous for a public sector career, since regardless of whether or not you work for a government agency or a non profit, all of these organizations exist within the broader political and governmental landscape, so understanding the basics of government and politics is crucial.

- **Public policy courses** are another area of study that could be worthwhile. These courses might be general public policy processes courses, they might be policy analysis and evaluation classes, or they might be topical areas of policy, such as healthcare policy or environmental policy. You should explore these courses as your interests dictate. For example, if you are thinking about a career path in working with at-risk youth populations, you might be interested in a social welfare policy course even if you are majoring in education. All public sector organizations are involved in public policy—especially the implementation of that policy—so courses in this area are helpful.

- **Organizations, leadership, and management courses** should probably be a part of everyone's college experience since virtually all career paths require working in organizations and working with other people. Classes in organizational theory and behavior and in management will be invaluable, whether or not you ultimately end up in the public sector. And leadership training is important—yet too few programs emphasize coursework in this area, particularly at the undergraduate level. There is much to be said for the practice of leadership, but there is also much to be said for studying leadership.

- **Ethics courses** are important and worth taking. It may be easy to think that you will always behave ethically when confronted with a challenging situation, but how do you know you will? Have you stopped to consider the difficulties of those situations and having to act quickly? Ethics courses can help you take the time you need to think through ethical dilemmas before you encounter them so you are prepared for them when you do. Ethics courses may be found in philosophy departments, but they are also likely found in many majors as well, such as business ethics. We live in a fast-paced world, and when we find ourselves in a challenging situation, it can be helpful if we've stopped and thought about what those situations look like before they happen.

- **Courses in economics and budgeting** may not be at the top of your list (although, as an economics major, I can tell you that the field is far more interesting than you might initially think!), but they are essential. The old adage that money makes the world go 'round is based in reality. Whatever you do professionally—and especially in the public sector—you need to have an understanding of the basics of the economy and how it works. And you need to know a bit about how budgeting in the public sector and organizations works.

- **Communication (oral and written) courses** are likely part of your institution's degree requirements, so you're probably taking them already, but it is worth mentioning that the ability to communicate well and professionally is essential. You should think about how the skills you're learning in English, writing, and communication courses will impact your professional work. In thinking about communication, you should look to take additional courses in areas that you feel could be strengthened through additional practice. These courses should also help you learn how to synthesize a lot of information and summarize it in a brief memo or other format.

By no means should you look at the list above as a checklist of courses you should take, nor should you look at this list and feel as though you have to take all of these courses, plus everything else required for your major. This list is meant to give you something to think about as you are selecting additional courses. For example, if you are required to take a course from a different school or unit on campus, perhaps look to the business school for a management course. Or, if you have to take a social science course, look to economics. For most people, college is the last time that they will formally take courses and study, but this shouldn't be the end of your learning. In fact, it should be the beginning of a life spent learning and growing. Use your time in college to take advantage of learning about things that are interesting to you, things that are outside of your major. As Carol Dweck, a psychology professor, describes well in her best-selling book *Mindset: The New Psychology of Success*, you should pursue a "growth mindset" rather than a "fixed mindset." A person with a growth mindset is always eager to learn more and learn about new things, whereas a person with a fixed mindset is perfectly content with what he or she already knows. Whatever you do after college, strive for a growth mindset. Cultivate your learning. Keep discovering. This attitude will serve you well whether or not you ultimately pursue a career in the public sector. And when you are taking courses for the remainder of your formal educational career, keep this emphasis on lifelong learning in mind.

Application Activity

In your last Application Activity, you investigated various degree programs your institution offers and sought additional information about those majors. For this activity, let's build on those efforts and explore your general education requirements and the flexibility you do have in the coursework for your major to select courses that will help you (1) figure out if the public sector is of interest to you and to (2) find courses that might help your pursuit of such a path.

First, access the requirements for major(s) and minor(s). Pull them up online, in your catalog, or write them out in front of you. Look at the list. What have you taken? What do you have left to take? For the courses that still remain, what options do you have? What flexibility do you have to pick classes that might enable you to determine whether the public sector is right for you? For example, if you are a political science major and you need to take courses in two of five political science subfields, take a course in public administration. Don't let the title of the course dissuade you—I know it doesn't sound fascinating—but public administration is all about how government agencies and non profit organizations carry out public policy—typically created by our elected leaders—and serve the public. Such a course, despite its title, will help you figure out if you continue to be interested in the sector.

Next, do the same for your general education requirements. What have you taken and what do you still need to take? In the areas that you still have requirements to fulfill, where might you plug in some courses that are interesting to you and may help prepare you for the public sector? If you are interested in working in the public sector and promoting economic development in your region, is there an interesting history course about the growth and development of labor unions? Or is there a course in economics and finance on economic development? Or, yet still, is there a course on promoting entrepreneurialism in the community?

Finally, peruse the entire listing of courses for the next academic semester when it's available. I realize that for some institutions, this could be a daunting order, but do it. There is no way to know what kinds of courses exist at your school unless you look. Personally, I continue to be surprised by the courses that we offer at my institution, and the list of courses that sound interesting to me that I want to take keeps growing—really! It is easy to assume that all physics courses must be an orderly sequence of courses titled Physics 1, 2, and so forth, but what else might that department offer? You never know until you look. Once you've gone through these requirements and taken a look, put together a list of courses that interest you and talk with your advisor and faculty members about them. And then be strategic in your course selections for the coming semesters and use those course slots to learn and develop skills that will help you in the public sector and foster a growth mindset.

USING YOUR COURSE ASSIGNMENTS AND ACTIVITIES

While it may seem difficult to link the work you are doing in a particular course this semester to your career path, it can be done (and with less effort than you might imagine) and you should capitalize on the opportunities to do so each term. In this final section, we are going to think about how to be strategic in using your course assignments to explore the public sector and how the activities you do for your classes can be used to build a portfolio and add to your resume as you look for internships, jobs, and even graduate school admissions.

Every course you take requires you to complete assignments and activities to help you learn the content and skills that are the goal of that course as well as help the instructor assess whether or not you have learned the material. There are many instances in which those assignments are very prescribed for you and there is little flexibility in them, but there are other cases in which you have a good deal of latitude—and you should utilize this latitude to keep exploring the public sector. For example, you may have the opportunity to research a policy area that you are interested in for a public policy course. You should pick something that you are interested in professionally, not just the topic that the instructor suggests. Go back to some of the activities in the first chapter and think about what areas of policy you are intrigued by and then delve into those areas to pick your research topic for the semester. If you aren't sure how to proceed, talk to your course instructor. I can assure you that faculty welcome the opportunity to help students pick topics that are of interest to them—believe me, you'll do a better job with a topic you're interested in and faculty can tell, making it far more enjoyable to read your work. Or perhaps you are in an ethics course and need to research a particular dilemma someone faced; again, use this opportunity to find a dilemma faced by someone in a public sector organization that is of interest to you and study the circumstances. Too often I see students pick topics for projects that are seemingly convenient rather than something that is fascinating to them. You have to do the assignment anyway, so you should maximize your efforts to both complete it and to find out more information about the public sector. Even if you aren't in a position to craft the assignment to align perfectly with what you want to learn and explore, do the best you can. Even if you have to pick from a list of topics for a research paper, think about how a topic on that list can help you learn more about an area or aspect of the public sector (or anything else for that matter) that you are interested in. Embracing this perspective when it comes to completing assignments will make them far more engaging and far less painful.

Class activities is another category of requirements for the courses you take. Often these activities can be group projects. While many students approach them with dread, you should remember that group activities are wonderful preparation for what your professional life will be like, and these activities offer you the opportunity to develop and hone skills that employers are interested in, such as building teams, leading, mentoring, problem solving, and collaborating to accomplish a task.

With all the assignments you complete and activities you engage in for your courses, keep in the back of your mind the notion that some of these efforts could prove worthy to include on your resume and in a portfolio for prospective employers or graduate admissions committees. Odds are that the next step in your professional career will entail applications and interviews, and many will ask for writing samples or other artifacts that demonstrate your knowledge, skills, and abilities. As you complete assignments and participate in activities, keep a literal or electronic folder in which you file them so you have them in one place when you need examples in the future. I cannot tell you how many times former students have gotten in touch with me to ask if I still had copies of this assignment or that policy paper years later because they need a writing assignment for an interview. Trust me, faculty may keep plenty of books and lots of paper in our offices, but we rarely hold on to student work for that length of time! Also, think about the skills you're developing, such as research abilities and effective group work practices, as resumes often include a section on skills. We'll talk a bit more about the skills you're refining in the next chapter, on co-curricular activities, too.

Application Activity

For the final Application Activity in this chapter, gather the syllabi for the courses you are taking this semester and review the assignments and activities you are required to complete. Make a list of the activities for which you might be able to propose your own topic or select a topic that enables you to dig into some of the areas of the public sector that you identified in the last chapter that are appealing to you. Which assignments might allow you to both find out more about something you're interested in and complete course requirements? Even if you cannot identify too many opportunities, remember Carol Dweck's emphasis on a growth mindset and think about what you are learning in those assignments and how that contributes to your growth and professional development.

Second, examine the work that you have done this semester and the work you will do, and make notes about what activities might be useful in the future as demonstrative of your skills. What assignments were particularly interesting and which are you are proud of? Which activities required effort that really shows how you've grown and learned over the semester? It is never too soon to tuck away some of those examples for the future.

CHAPTER WRAP-UP

In this chapter, we have explored the curricular components of your college career. First, we considered selection of majors and reminded you that work in the public sector does not require a degree in political science; instead, there are career paths available to you for any major you select. And it's important to remember that your choice of a major is just that, *your choice*. You should major in an area that you are interested in and are excited about since you're the one who has to do the work and complete the requirements.

Taking courses is an essential part of your college career, and they should be thought of as having multiple purposes beyond completing requirements on a course checklist or degree audit. And the courses you take, both as part of your major and outside of your major, can also help you investigate various aspects of the public sector and compile examples of your work for portfolios and writing samples that you might need to submit as part of applications and interviews in the future.

ACTION ITEMS

After reading this chapter, you should have (1) identified programs of study or academic majors that are interesting to you, (2) noted courses that seem intriguing and might help meet various major and general education requirements, and (3) thought about how the activities and assignments you must do in your courses can help you explore the public sector, learn new things, and provide examples of your abilities for portfolios and inclusion on your resume. Pulling together this information will help make the day-to-day experiences of your courses more meaningful and help you figure out if the public sector is something you want to pursue professionally.

PUBLIC SECTOR PROFILE

Emily Kaylor, Chief of Staff, Office of Ohio Lieutenant Governor Mary Taylor

Emily Kaylor earned a Bachelor of Arts degree in political science with a minor in history from the University of Dayton and then went on to earn a Master of Public Administration degree from Indiana University. Currently, she is the chief of staff for Mary Taylor, lieutenant governor of Ohio.

1. **What is your current job and how did your studies prepare you for this role? How does that job align with what you thought you'd be doing when you were in college?**

   My current job is chief of staff to Ohio Lt. Governor Mary Taylor. My studies have greatly prepared me for this role. Particularly my graduate degree has helped with managing a staff of about 12 people of all different ages and backgrounds. My undergraduate degree has helped me navigate the legislative process, relationship building, and politics. Honestly, I never thought I'd be here when I was in college.

I expected to go to law school and practice law somewhere. I always liked the idea of public service but never imagined being in such a political role.

2. **What were some of the classes that really stood out to you in school that were influential in finding your career path?**

Legislative Politics with Governor Taft was a huge influence. He exposed me to the legislative process and so many individuals associated with state and federal government that it opened my eyes to new opportunities. Intro to Public Administration was also very influential as I learned the basic theories behind public administration and what careers in public service can be like. In grad school, Social Policy was actually very influential on me. I learned a lot of different perspectives on social policy and how to talk about difficult issues with people that you don't agree with to get to a policy goal.

3. **What are some classes you wish you took now that you didn't take or didn't have the chance to take in college?**

It would have been helpful to have a specific state government class but every state is so unique that I'm not sure it's really possible to have one of those. Honestly, I feel my education prepared me very well and the only classes I wish I had taken were more electives in history, criminal justice, political science, sociology, and other subjects but there was only so much time.

4. **What internships and/or co-curricular activities did you participate in, and how did they prepare you for your graduate work and/or professional trajectory?**

The two activities that stand out for my career path were UD's Student Government Association and the UD Statehouse Civic Scholar internship program. The internship program was in Columbus and was really my first experience with state government, where I have ended up for now. Student Government taught me a lot about leadership, politics, and conflict as I served as president senior year after a long campaign.

5. **What advice would you give to your undergraduate self? Or, in other words, what do you wish you knew as an undergraduate that you know now?**

I would tell my undergraduate self to take advantage of alumni and other individuals willing to participate in internships or shadow opportunities. I was so narrowly focused on law school I didn't realize the opportunities until later in my collegiate career. I would also say that grades don't matter as much as learning. People are much more interested in hearing about your experience and growth than about what classes you got an A in.

CHAPTER THREE

CO-CURRICULAR OPPORTUNITIES AND EXPERIENCES

In college, you spend a lot of time in classes and you spend a lot of time thinking about your courses, but that is only part of the learning experience. Learning does not just happen in the classroom; learning also occurs through a variety of other experiences, often labeled co-curricular experiences. In this chapter, we explore the range of opportunities that encompass co-curricular experiences, and we discuss what opportunities you should consider pursuing as you weigh a future in the public sector. More specifically, in this chapter we will

- define co-curricular opportunities and discuss why they are important— even essential—to your college career,

- talk about how to pursue these opportunities and how they can help you decide if the public sector is right for you and give you experiences beyond the classroom that enhance your future in the public sector, and

- reflect on what can be learned from co-curricular experiences that may not fulfill expectations for a host of reasons.

Here we not only consider all the wonderful aspects of co-curricular opportunities, but we also reflect on what to do when the perfect experience does not present itself or the seemingly amazing internship may not live up to expectations. It is worth remembering that we can and do learn from all of these experiences—and they can still help you find the right fit for you in the public sector. At the conclusion of this chapter, you should have a good understanding of co-curricular opportunities, how to pursue them, and what you might learn from them.

WHAT ARE CO-CURRICULAR OPPORTUNITIES AND EXPERIENCES?

The term *co-curricular* is common on a college campus, but its actual meaning and examples are often vague and even confusing. Co-curricular refers to the activities, programs, and opportunities that are learning experiences and are connected to your curriculum but not necessarily the academic courses that you receive academic credit for—although you may receive credit in some instances. In many cases, these activities take place on campus and/or are sponsored or sanctioned by your university. Co-curricular activities are different than extra curricular activities in that the latter often are not connected to your academic course of study. For example, co-curricular activities include academic organizations (e.g., Model United Nations or Mock Trial), service organizations (e.g., service clubs), internship and co-op experiences, education abroad, and independent research endeavors.

Some of these opportunities do not have academic credit attached to them, such as service organizations or Mock Trial, but they can offer you opportunities to engage in topics closely related to the public sector. Mock Trial, for example, could be invaluable if you are thinking about a career in the public defender's office and want to gain insights into what it might be like to be a practicing attorney trying a case. Service organizations might offer you the chance to work with various populations in your community that may be in need of or are benefiting from social services that demonstrate social policy and government in action. These opportunities might also enable you to see how a non profit organization works from the inside. More and more universities are including these sorts of activities on companion transcripts that accompany your formal academic transcript. You should ask your advisor or check with the registrar's office as to whether or not your campus provides one of these transcripts. Co-curricular transcripts serve as official documentation of some of these alternative learning experiences that you have had while pursuing your academic degree.

Internships are invaluable in anyone's career exploration, not just in the public sector. And pursuing these opportunities cannot be emphasized enough. For some students at some institutions, internships can come with academic credit, and in other cases, they may not. Either way, you should give serious thought to pursuing several internships over the course of your college career. And it's important to note that internships come in all sizes and shapes and in locations everywhere across the country—they aren't just the congressional internships that seem to be the obvious choice for political science majors. You might intern in a local law firm or with a state environmental agency or with the U.S. Department of State or any one of the other thousands of public sector organizations. There are lots of organizations that help connect students to opportunities in the public sector ranging from state government internship programs to the Partnership for Public Service (https://ourpublicservice.org/). It's worth remembering that an internship can help you figure out what you want to do professionally and can also—and perhaps more importantly—help you figure out what you don't want to do as well! For example, you may have a great internship working in your local public health department but decide that isn't for you. And that's perfectly fine, and it's still a good experience.

Some co-curricular activities do come with academic credit, such as education abroad programs and independent research opportunities. *Education abroad* is the umbrella term that is used for study abroad opportunities in other countries and even opportunities domestically. They can be provided through your own university or an affiliated university and may last for a semester, an entire year, or may be shorter in duration, such as an abbreviated summer or winter term. In addition to the academic course work that typically accompanies these programs, students participating in these opportunities benefit from cultural and language immersion. These programs might enable you to take courses in government and policy that you might not have the opportunity to take on your campus, and they might offer you a chance to work with a non profit or other government entity while abroad to help you explore what a career in the public sector might look like. For example, studying abroad in Cape Town, South Africa, might afford you the chance to take courses in how that country's government works and the challenges its public sector takes from people with firsthand experiences in it. And there might be an opportunity to intern with a public sector organization dedicated to thwarting poaching of the nation's rhinoceros population.

Research projects are often a staple of some of your courses, particularly upper-division courses, but independent research projects, such as a thesis or directed research with a faculty member, are efforts done outside of the classroom that can be invaluable. Perhaps you have a nagging question about the effectiveness of a particular government policy or whether or not television shows portray government bureaucrats in a certain way. These sorts of questions can prompt independent research that, while challenging, can be extremely rewarding. And if you do not have a specific question that you want to research, odds are good that a faculty member of yours does and would welcome help with those research efforts. You don't have to be a graduate student or a professor to conduct original research! These research opportunities can help you peek into the world of policy analysis or some other aspect of the public sector as you contemplate a career in it.

Our discussion so far has focused on the different types of co-curricular experiences you might pursue that relate to the public sector in specific ways, but we should also consider how these opportunities can enhance your education while you are in school and contribute to your future success more generally. First, co-curricular experiences allow you to delve more deeply into areas that you are interested in and subjects you may be passionate about. Literacy may be a particular area of focus for you; you may volunteer with an organization that strives to improve adult literacy, and you may work with a faculty member in sociology, teacher education, or political science to study the effectiveness of public sector actions to promote literacy. It is one thing to be interested about a given topic in the classroom and quite another to be interested in action related to it. This leads to a second benefit of these activities: They offer the opportunity to apply what you're learning in the classroom, and they complement academic learning. Whether it is a math problem in your statistics class or reading a policy paper, having to do it yourself is something quite different. Co-curricular experiences can give you the chance to run statistical tests on your own data and to answer the research questions you are interested in, not just those set forth in a problem set assigned by your professor. And an internship with a government agency or local non profit organization could give you the opportunity to write a policy paper and advocate for a public policy solution that you are passionate about. Third, these opportunities can establish a foundation for your professional life and give you tangible and real-world experiences to talk about as you apply for jobs and/or graduate school. These experiences translate into skills for your resume and future applications; consider the following:

- Working with others translates into the skills of teamwork and collaboration.

- Giving talks or presenting information translates into public speaking and oral communication skills.

- Reading and conducting research translates into analytical and critical thinking skills.

- Engaging many people on complex tasks in a club or organization translates into project management skills.

- Studying abroad or working with diverse populations can translate into intercultural competence skill development.

Some people may tell you that participating in co-curricular opportunities may divert your attention from your academics, and while this can be a valid consideration, you should think about what you can gain from the co-curricular experiences that enhance your academics. And these opportunities to apply what you're learning in the classroom and to gain experience will help you figure out if a career in the public sector is right for you.

Application Activity

For the first Application Activity of this chapter, let's do some brainstorming. We've talked about different types of co-curricular experiences, including campus groups and organizations, internships, education abroad, and independent research. Do the following brainstorming exercises for each of the categories of co-curricular opportunities and write down your responses to each of the questions:

- For campus groups and organizations, what are two types of groups you're interested in finding out more about? Why?

- For internship opportunities, what are two types of organizations you'd like to work for or what are two issue areas you'd like to work in?

- For education abroad, what are two subjects you'd like to study abroad?

- For independent research, what are two topics that you'd like to research? Or what are two classes that you found particularly fascinating and you'd like to talk with the professor about opportunities to conduct research in those topics areas?

After you've done this brainstorming, review what you've written down and see if there are overlaps between your ideas and the public sector. Use the areas of overlap as a guide for where to do some searching regarding next steps.

PURSUING CO-CURRICULAR EXPERIENCES

The previous section helped clarify what is encompassed by the term *co-curricular* and what kinds of experiences you might be interested in, particularly as they pertain to pursuing a public sector career. This section follows up on those broad conversations by offering tips about how to pursue these opportunities.

First, you have to be proactive, you have to look early, and you always have to keep an eye open for co-curricular opportunities. These points may seem commonsensical, but experience suggests it's worth repeating. Regardless of whether you are pursuing education abroad opportunities or want to intern in your hometown, you are the one who has to seek out those prospects. And you can't wait until the last minute either. If you are looking for a summer internship, your best bet is to start looking in January—I know that seems early, but hiring employees, even interns, takes time and requires approvals, so organizations start early. And even if you contact the local parks district in your community and they haven't quite figured out how many interns they'll be hiring and what projects they will tackle just yet, it's good to give them your resume and for them to know your name for when you do apply. When it comes to education abroad, this can take even more planning because fitting in all your required courses, especially if you're a double major, often necessitates careful planning to keep you on track to your target graduation date. For instance, if you are looking at an opportunity in St. Petersburg, Russia, and there you'll take several history courses that can count for your general education requirements, don't take history courses on your institution's campus; fulfill other requirements instead. Additionally, the likelihood that organizations on campus will come knocking on your door asking you to join is probably low, so you need to explore the opportunities available to you through your campus's student involvement office and website and reach out to the leaders of those organizations you're interested in.

Without a doubt, looking early for opportunities and being proactive may not be the easiest thing to do and it can often be the first thing that gets pushed aside with the day-to-day realities of the semester. But the bottom line is you have to make time for these activities—to spend time looking for opportunities and reaching out to organizations and inquiring about options. It does take work, but in the end, it will be worth it and these experiences will help you figure out what's right for you in the future. And this brings us to another important point.

Second, it is essential that you talk to a lot of people—and keep talking to them! No matter what you end up doing in your career, your professional network is essential and you start building it when you're in college. My professional network got its start when I was in college and graduate school, and decades later, those contacts are still the foundation of my network.

We have talked in previous chapters about the importance of talking to others about their paths and getting their advice; in the context of co-curricular experiences, you should also talk to them about opportunities they may know about and find out if they know of any opportunities that might be right for you. In terms of thinking about co-curricular activities that might help you think about a public sector career, you should talk to the following people:

- Your faculty members should know about opportunities on campus and be able to draw on their own experiences and paths of students before you.

- Your advisor should be helpful in figuring out requirements and keeping you on track to graduate as well as get you ready for your career after you've earned your degree.

- Staff in your institution's career services office can tell you about internship experiences in particular since their job is to help you get ready for your career.

- Alumni from your department and university can be invaluable and are often overlooked; ask in your department and in career services about getting in touch with recent alumni who are working in areas that you are interested in, and reach out to them and talk. It might sound strange talking to a stranger about career paths, but you already have a shared college experience that will help "break the ice," and I cannot tell you how often alumni want to help current students because invariably other alumni helped them.

- Friends and family members are also a great source of input and support.

- Even cold call (or email) specific individuals in public sector organizations that you are interested in. Don't necessarily email generic inboxes for an organization, but look for specific people to connect with, to explain who you are and what you're interested in. You may not always get a response, but you definitely won't get a response if you don't try. You will be surprised at how often people do want to help.

Application Activity

Given our conversation in this section, it should come as no surprise that this Application Activity is focused on identifying people to talk with about co-curricular opportunities. Make a list of five people that you want to talk with about whatever kind of co-curricular experience you want to have. List five individuals who you respect and perhaps find their career paths and experiences interesting. Pull the contact information for the individuals as well. Then for each of the five people, write down three questions you want to ask each of them. When you're done, you should have 15 questions ready to go! Then, send emails or call the five people and ask them if they have a few minutes to talk with you. When you hear back from them, you'll be all set with your questions to start the conversation. And it's often a good idea to ask these individuals about the co-curricular experiences they may have had or the ones they wish they had. There is often valuable advice to be had in these sorts of conversations!

REFLECTING ON SUCCESSFUL AND LESS SUCCESSFUL CO-CURRICULAR EXPERIENCES

Guides like this one often stop at the end of the last section in describing what kinds of opportunities you might avail yourself of and how to find them. We should take that conversation a step further here and point out that sometimes these experiences are fantastic and pivotal for the rest of your professional life and sometimes they are not. In the best of circumstances, an independent research experience with a faculty member might help you figure out the area of policy that you are passionate about and will spend the rest of your life studying and working in or an internship may solidify your desire to work for a state environmental agency. Or they may not. You may work with a faculty member and discover you don't like that area of research that much, or you may realize after a summer internship that you don't want to work in a law firm. These latter experiences are just as important as the former. Co-curricular experiences will help you figure out what you love just as much as they will help you figure out what you loathe—and it's better to find out the latter sooner rather than later!

Whatever you do in your professional life, you should foster a reflective practice, like Donald Schön detailed in his book *The Reflective Practitioner*. During and after a co-curricular experience, take time to think about what is going well and what is not going well. Be honest with yourself and think about why. If you aren't finding an internship experience with a local non profit organization all that fulfilling, why not? It may be easy to blame the organization or say it's not a good fit, but why isn't it? Why isn't it motivating to you? What, if anything, are you doing (or not doing) that may be making it worse? I'm reminded of the advice Nigel (played by Stanley Tucci) gives Andy (portrayed by Anne Hathaway) in the movie *The Devil Wears Prada* when Andy is trying to cope with being an assistant to the powerful fashion editor Miranda Priestly (depicted by Meryl Streep) even though she detests the industry. Nigel says, "Andy, be serious. You are not trying. You are whining." Andy comes to realize that she needs to change her mindset about the work, and when she does, it becomes more rewarding. Keeping this advice in mind throughout your professional life will serve you well.

CHAPTER WRAP-UP

In this chapter, we have discussed how co-curricular experiences can enhance your time in college and how they can help you figure out what kind of career in the public sector might be right for you. You should think about all of these opportunities as a chance to figure out if there are aspects of the public sector that you find intriguing and could see yourself pursuing a career in. And there are a lot of people to help you in these pursuits; you just have to ask.

ACTION ITEMS

After reading this chapter, you should have (1) a working definition of co-curricular opportunities, (2) identified some opportunities you are interested in possibly pursuing, and (3) thought about how to pursue those opportunities, including who you should talk to as a first step.

PUBLIC SECTOR PROFILE

Geenae Rivera Soto, Policy Analyst, Federal Housing Finance Agency[1]

Geenae Rivera Soto is a policy analyst, specializing in single-family markets, for the Federal Housing Finance Agency in Washington, D.C. She double-majored at the University of Dayton, earning a degree in political science and Spanish. Then, she went on to earn two master's degrees, one in public administration from the University of Dayton and one in city and regional planning from Catholic University of America.

1. **What is your current job and how did your studies prepare you for this role? How does that job align with what you thought you'd be doing when you were in college?**

---

[1] Disclaimer: The replies to these questions are Ms. Geenae Rivera Soto's own and do not necessarily represent the views of her agency. She contributed to this Q and A in her personal capacity.

My current job is a policy analyst in a financial regulatory federal agency. My agency is legally required to implement requirements specified in the Federal Housing Enterprises Financial Safety and Soundness Act of 1992, as amended by the Housing and Economic Recovery Act of 2008. Part of the statute requires Fannie Mae and Freddie Mac to provide leadership to facilitate a secondary market for mortgages on housing for very low-, low-, and moderate-income families in three undeserved markets: manufactured housing, affordable housing preservation, and rural housing. My division oversees this program.

My studies prepared me for this role by helping me develop good analytical and problem solving skills and having a basic understanding of government and how it functions.

The job does not align at all with what I thought I would be doing in college. When I was in college I had planned on attending law school and practicing law. Even though I was a political science major I had a heavy focus on international relations. I thought I would go to law school and eventually work in foreign policy issues or immigration issues.

2. **What were some of the classes that really stood out to you in school that were influential in finding your career path?**

I definitely had some classes that stood out for me and had a big impact, but I cannot truly say that any were influential in finding my career path. My career path had a life of its own outside of my academic interests/paths. My career path was more guided by an internship I did in the summer between graduating college and starting graduate school. I had the opportunity to participate in a Hispanic leadership program called the Congressional Hispanic Leadership Institute. Through this program, I interned in Congress for the member from Puerto Rico. After this experience, I knew I wanted to work in government and come back to D.C. after I was done with school. I was not sure where I wanted to work or where I would end up, but I knew that my career path was decided as a public servant. This program is what truly shaped my career path.

My education definitely helped me along the way as I experienced different jobs, first with a non profit, then in Congress, and finally at the federal agency where I work today. Some of the classes that I found most influential in undergraduate were Developmental Political Theory, Constitutional Law, U.S. National Security Policy, and Urban Politics. These four classes gave me a good basis for understanding political theory, how the federal government operates and functions in terms of policy at the national and international level, and finally how local and state government operate. In my MPA program, some of the classes that stood out were Government Planning and State and Local Government. These two classes gave me a good understanding of local and state government at a micro level and were my inspiration for continuing my studies later on in urban planning. In my MCRP program, some of the classes that stood out were Politics and Planning, Urban Economics, and my thesis work/study. These two courses along with my thesis gave me a good basis for understanding planning, at both the local and national levels, but also to focus on affordable housing and how to develop programs that benefit those most in need.

3. What are some classes you wish you took now that you didn't take or didn't have the chance to take in college?

I wish I had taken some introductory courses in finance. As pertaining to my current job this would have been very helpful to have some basic understanding of the financial industry, especially the secondary mortgage industry.

4. What internships and/or co-curricular activities did you participate in and how did they prepare you for your graduate work and/or professional trajectory?

As I mentioned before, the main internship program that really shaped me and prepared me for my professional trajectory was participating in the Congressional Hispanic Leadership Institute's internship. I participated in a summer internship in Washington, D.C., between finishing my undergraduate degree and doing the master in public administration. I was placed in former Congressman Luis Fortuño's office from Puerto Rico. This program definitely set me for a career in public service just by the exposure I received by interning in Congress and all the different educational activities the program provided. Nevertheless, not to a lesser degree all my professors at the University of Dayton both for undergrad and graduate school (some of which overlapped) were very encouraging and always provided guidance on the possibility of becoming a public servant.

5. What advice would you give to your undergraduate self? Or, in other words, what do you wish you knew as an undergraduate that you know now?

The advice I would give to my undergraduate self would be to do more studying abroad, to take some intro finance or business classes, and to take career risks when the opportunity came along right after graduation. Not to be so scared of the unknown as I was starting my professional career. It is easier to make riskier moves right after college than the older you get when you have more responsibilities.

CHAPTER FOUR

FINDING YOUR PASSION AND PURSUING IT

During the course of your college career, you've probably been told by someone that college comprises the best years of your life, so you should make the most of it. Although that comment is usually well intentioned—and we won't debate whether or not it's true—that comment can be stress inducing. After all, it is during these college years that there's pressure to figure it all out. And that's easier said than done! So far in this volume, we've discussed what is actually meant by the term *public sector* and the range of career possibilities it holds. We've explored the academic courses in your college curriculum that may enable you to think about those career options. And we've also considered how co-curricular opportunities can help you both discern what public sector pathway might be right for you and enhance your start by having some of these experiences before you complete your degree.

In this final chapter, we take a step back and talk about finding your passions and learning beyond college because college is not the end; it's just the beginning. And that means all those stress-inducing decisions that seemingly have to be made by the time you earn your degree aren't really as final or permanent as they seem to be. College is just another step on your path. And if you asked other people to be honest, the vast majority of them would say they didn't have it all figured out in college either. More specifically, in this chapter we will

- discuss finding your passions and letting those passions drive your career pursuits,

- be mindful that learning does not stop when you receive your degree at commencement and talk about what learning can look like in the future—both in the pursuit of additional degrees and in the more informal professional development you will engage in your entire career, and

- offer some summary insights about the next phase of your life.

At the conclusion of this chapter, you will have had the opportunity to reflect on what motivates you professionally and how to keep that excitement alive in your career. It's easy to think that you have to have it all figured out, but rest assured, regardless of whether or not you pursue a career in the public sector, you will figure it out.

FINDING YOUR PASSIONS

Underlying much of our discussion in the earlier chapters was figuring out what you are interested in and how those interests might lead to a meaningful career in the public sector. As you think about your professional aspirations, it is essential to keep your passions as the driving force behind those decisions. And it is worth recognizing that decisions aren't final. Choices you make now about your major and even your first job do not have to define the rest of your working life—indeed, changing careers is very common. Interests evolve over time. Just like when you were younger, you may have wanted to do one thing with your life and then, over time, those interests morphed.

In thinking about your passions, you should also ponder two key questions: (1) What do you want to do with your life? (2) What kind of person are you? These questions should be at the foundation of your decision making, not what other people in your life tell you that you should do or what you think will be the right career path for you. What is it you want to do with your life? How do you want to strive for meaning and joy in your life? How do you want to serve and whom do you want to serve? Responses to these questions should be considered alongside reflections about yourself. What kind of person are you? What are your gifts and talents? What are your passions? These are definitely not easy questions nor are they questions that elicit a quick and concise response. And that's all right; that's how it should be.

Application Activity

It's one thing to read the words above and pay passing attention to the answers to these questions, but it's another thing to spend some time articulating a response to them. Accordingly, for the first Application Activity of this chapter, spend some time thinking about the following questions and writing down your responses. It might be particularly helpful to keep a file on your computer or other electronic device of your responses, or even write down your thoughts on a piece of paper or in a notebook. However you decide to capture your thoughts right now, it's worthwhile to keep those notes someplace where you can refer to them from time to time.

First, let's begin with questions about your interests and passions. Write down answers to the following questions:

- What do you like to do? Why do you like to do those things?

- What are your passions?

Next, think about who you are. Write down answers to the following questions:

- What are you good at? You have strengths. What are some of those strengths?
- What are your gifts and talents?
- How do you want to make the world a better place?

And, finally, see if you can connect your responses to both sets of questions. Collect your reflections to the questions above and think about where you might be able to make a contribution. What is something that you could pursue professionally—perhaps in the public sector or perhaps not—that ignites your passions, harnesses your strengths, and will offer meaning for you in life? Is there overlap between your passions, strengths, and something that would provide fulfillment for you in life? The intersection of those responses is where you'll find your career path and meaning in your life.

LEARNING BEYOND COLLEGE

College does not represent the end of your learning nor does it represent your final decision of what you will do professionally. In fact, college is just a step along the way. And even if it seems like college is the end of your formal schooling, it's not. The fact of the matter is that you can and should continue to learn throughout your professional life, and that learning can take formal paths such as additional degrees or certificates, or other professional development pursuits. And learning should also include discovering something new every day in informal settings and interactions. Hopefully, instead of this revelation inducing fear, it should ease some of the anxiety associated with the selection of courses, majors, and even early professional experiences. Remember our discussions in Chapter 2 about cultivating a "growth mindset" rather than a "fixed mindset." Remember you're always learning and that learning can take you down different paths—be open to it.

Professional development will likely be a required part of any job, and it's absolutely essential to a productive and fulfilling career. You have probably already experienced some training and the desire to advance in the jobs you have held or currently hold. Whether it's working in a movie theater and wanting to get trained to sell tickets instead of having to scoop popcorn, most advancement requires training. Attending workshops and training programs in your organization and through other groups, such as professional organizations, will be a mainstay of your career. If you hold a law license, you have to maintain that license by attending lectures, workshops, or other training opportunities each year. This ensures that you stay up-to-date with current topics and the latest advances in your field.

Conferences also provide the chance to learn and engage in your field. In the public sector, some of the major organizations, including the American Society for Public Administration (http://www.aspanet.org), the International City/County Management Association (http://icma.org), and the Association for Research on Nonprofit Organizations and Voluntary Action (http://www.arnova.org), are just a few of the organizations for public sector professionals that cut across areas of expertise. Then within a particular area—such as national security or intelligence—there are many more organizations. The point is your learning can and should continue long after you leave your college campus. And all of these opportunities also enable you to network and talk with other people in your field.

Graduate degrees are another, more formal way to continue learning beyond those professional development activities described above. When it comes to the public sector, a range of graduate degrees are common, including master's degrees and doctoral degrees—especially law degrees. Broadly speaking, master's degrees encompass around 30 to 40 additional semester hours, or about 10 to 12 classes. Unlike your undergraduate degree, master's degrees typically only require coursework in your field of study—so, in other words, no general education classes. Graduate academic work is more intensive than your undergraduate courses, so completing a master's degree is likely to take you three or four semesters of full-time coursework. Doctoral degrees require about three times the amount of semester hours than master's degrees do, although there is wide variety in their requirements. Doctoral degrees are terminal degrees and imply that the individuals who have earned them are experts in some aspect of their field of study. Most of your college professors likely have doctoral degrees. These degrees require years of additional coursework, then there are usually formal exams that have to be passed, and then there is the dissertation, which is a massive research project that has to be conducted and submitted for review. Law degrees, or juris doctorates (JD), are a type of doctoral degree, but are different than doctorate of philosophy—or PhD—degrees. JDs entail three years of full-time coursework beyond undergraduate degrees. Earning a JD doesn't require exams or a dissertation the way most PhD programs do, but to earn a law license, one has to take the bar exam.

In addition to the graduate degrees discussed, in recent years, graduate certificates are emerging as another formal credentialing option. Universities offer graduate certificates, which often range from three to five graduate courses, in a particular area. For example, a graduate certificate may be sought in non-profit management or sustainability studies. Earning this certificate would signal to others that you have advanced graduate work in these specific areas beyond your undergraduate degree. But these certificates do not carry the same weight as a master's degree. At many institutions, graduate certificates may also be earned alongside a graduate degree.

After discussing the kinds of formal degree programs available, we need to consider some of the fields of study that are particularly useful in the public sector. In addition to advanced degrees in subjects and disciplines you're probably familiar with from your undergraduate experience, including mathematics, engineering, biology, history, communication, and so forth, there are a number of fields of graduate study that are particularly useful for the public sector; these fields include public administration, public policy, and urban and regional planning. Public administration is the study of how government and the public sector does what it does—how government and non profit organizations implement the decisions of our elected leaders. This field focuses on how a law, such as the Clean Water Act, may be implemented by the federal Environmental Protection Agency, along with efforts by state and local government environmental agencies. In other words, public administration is concerned with the "doing" of government. Master of Public Administration (MPA) degrees are very much like Master of Business Administration (MBA) degrees in terms of the kinds and ranges of courses (e.g., organization theory and behavior, ethics, leadership, management, budgeting and finance), but MPAs are focused on government and non profit organizations rather than for-profit corporations. Unlike MBAs, students in MPA programs will also take courses in public policy, which focus on how the public problems find their way to the agendas of elected leaders and how any decisions that are made are implemented, and how we know if policies are succeeding. These degrees offer you the management and executive training you need in the public sector. Public policy is such a rich area of study that you can also earn a Master of Public Policy (MPP) degree as well. MPPs focus on the creation of public policy and methods to evaluate whether or not a policy is "working." Another area of study, urban and regional planning, focuses on how land is used and developed. Planners help communities grow, develop, and revitalize land and facilities in a community. Ultimately, graduate degrees provide you specialized training in an area that can be advantageous to your professional pursuits, but they are generally not required, particularly for entry-level jobs.

If you are interested in graduate degrees, there are several things to think about. First, you should consider whether you want to pursue a degree like an MPA or MPP that sets you up to work in a range of areas in the public sector. Directors of non profit organizations and budget analysts in a local government would both benefit from an MPA. But in those areas, you may wish to earn a degree in a more focused area, such as finance or engineering, depending on the kind of work you want to do. It should come as no surprise to you that you should spend time talking to people in the fields you are thinking about working in and getting their take on what kind of graduate degree might make sense for you. A common topic for many in the public sector—particularly those who want to work as aides to elected leaders of government—is whether or not a law degree is essential. There is no simple answer to that question. To figure that out, you need to explore what dimension of public service you're interested in and see what may make sense for you. Besides talking with other people in the area, it can also be advantageous to peruse job ads and get a sense of the requirements, in terms of both educational backgrounds and workplace experience, that they seek. Take a look at ads for positions that you aspire to do, not just the ones you want to apply for now. This may help give you a sense of what kinds of degrees might be essential, not to mention the kinds of opportunities that you may be interested in pursuing in the future.

Second, another question is typically when to pursue graduate school. Again, there isn't a set answer. Sometimes it may make sense to pursue graduate school upon completing an undergraduate degree, especially law school. But in other cases, it may be worth exploring the public sector professionally for a few years and then returning to school on a part-time basis to earn a certificate or master's degree, for instance. Spending some time working may help you crystalize what you may want to study further rather than jumping straight into a graduate program that may be of less interest to you. Rest assured, graduate degrees can be earned in a variety of ways, from day classes to night classes to online programs.

Whatever you end up deciding about graduate degrees now or in the future, remember learning does not end with your undergraduate degree. Embrace Carol Dweck's "growth mindset" and always search for and take advantages of opportunities to learn. Those opportunities might be as simple as reading books after college. According to the Pew Research Center, nearly a quarter of Americans (24 percent) report that they haven't read a whole or even part of a book in the last year (and this includes audio books; Perrin 2018)!

Application Activity

The emphasis in this section has been on learning opportunities beyond college, and those opportunities might be informal, or professional development opportunities, or graduate degree programs. For this Application Activity, spend some time looking at job postings in the public sector and seek out opportunities that may not be entry-level, but are rather positions that you aspire to in the course of your career. One site, organized by the American Society for Public Administration, is http://www.publicservicecareers.org. If you are interested in local government, try ICMA's Job Center at https://icma.org/job-posts. And if you are intrigued by jobs in the federal government, check out https://www.usajobs.gov/. Or use your favorite search tool to look for jobs in a particular aspect of the public sector or in a geographic area you are interested in.

Once you've started browsing these positions, find three that are fascinating to you. For each of the three postings, answer the following questions: (1) What about the job description sparks your interest? (2) What does the position require? (3) What qualifications must you have to get the job? Note the kinds of background and educational requirements outlined in the post. Now write down the kinds of training or education you think would be advantageous for these positions and do some research as to some of the opportunities you might pursue for the kind of work described in these posts.

SUMMARY INSIGHTS

It can be very overwhelming to think about many of the topics we've covered in this chapter, and in this volume. So, this final section offers a few summary insights as you navigate your professional future and think about the public sector. These insights can be summed up as patience, grit, and reflection.

In today's world, patience can be hard with the readily available and nonstop information at our fingertips. Social media ensures that we know what people are doing all the time, professionally and socially. These realities can create a sense of urgency that we have to have things figured out and that we have to move on our decisions immediately. However, it is also important to be patient, and most importantly, be patient with yourself. It's ok not to know exactly what you want to do with your professional life, it's ok to try something and not like it, and it's ok to need time to figure things out. The vast majority of us need time to figure out what we want in our careers, and those wants may change over time.

In addition to patience, grit is also extremely important. Angela Duckworth is a psychology professor whose book *Grit: The Power of Passion and Perseverance* speaks eloquently about the need to try things and keep at it. We will spend our careers trying new things and we may or may not get it right the first time. This can be tough. Duckworth describes the need to try something and try it again, and to keep at it—to persevere. And sometimes, we may never become great at something, but we learn a lot in the process of trying and there is much that we will become great at. Much like patience, fostering grit can be hard in our society as it seemingly has little space for us to try something and fail. Much like we learned in grade school, how do we know if we're good at something or if we like something until we try?

A final, and related, insight is reflection. We've talked in previous chapters about the importance of reflecting on experiences and being honest with ourselves about what worked well and what didn't work as we had hoped it might. And it's worth underscoring the importance of reflection in your professional life, whether that ends up being in the public sector or not. It's one thing to try something, such as a new course or a job in a different area, but to get the most out of that experience, we have to think about and honestly reflect on what has gone well and where changes might be necessary. This reflective practice fosters growth.

As you look to your professional life, remember patience, grit, and reflection. All of these traits will be important as you spend the rest of your careers—and your lives—learning and pursuing your passions.

CHAPTER WRAP-UP

This chapter has focused on how to find your passions and how to find your professional paths. Our discussion has emphasized the need to figure out what it is that excites you and to let that be your guide in your professional endeavors. And it's worth remembering that those interests and passions may change, and that is perfectly acceptable. There is no rule that says you have to have it all figured out in college—most of us would be in big trouble if such a rule existed! College is just one part of your lifelong journey of learning, and that learning may continue in formal degree programs or it may take place in reading books and attending seminars in your community. The point is that learning is an ongoing process that doesn't end with college. Finally, the importance of patience, grit, and reflection were underscored as you think about what comes next for you professionally.

ACTION ITEMS

After reading this chapter, you should have (1) thought about where your passions lie today and (2) considered opportunities for learning beyond college. In the spirit of those points, you should look to additional resources as you consider careers in the public sector. The following websites and books are good places to continue those efforts:

- Partnership for Public Service (http://ourpublicservice.org)

- Public Service Stories (http://www.publicservicestories.com)

- Charles Goodsell's *The New Case for Bureaucracy* (2015, CQ Press)

- Mary Guy and Todd Ely's *Essentials of Public Service: An Introduction to Contemporary Public Administration* (2018 Melvin & Leigh).

PUBLIC SECTOR PROFILES

Cordell Williams, Grants and Development Administrator, Greater Dayton Premier Management, and Jennifer Pautz, Director of Government Affairs, New York University[1]

Cordell Williams is a grants and development administrator working in the local community in Dayton, Ohio. His undergraduate degree is in organizational leadership from Wright State University, and he earned a Master of Public Administration degree from the University of Dayton.

1. **What is your current job and how did your studies prepare you for this role? How does that job align with what you thought you'd be doing when you were in college?**

---

[1] Disclaimer: The replies to these questions are Mr. Cordell Williams's and Ms. Jennifer Pautz's own and do not necessarily represent the views of their agencies. They contributed to this Q and A in their personal capacities.

I'm currently working at the Dayton Metropolitan Housing Authority and Greater Dayton Premier Management as a grants and development administrator. I believe my undergraduate studies prepared me for this job through the multidisciplinary curriculum reviewing various industries and best practices for its leader. I explored the roles of leaders in the private and public sectors exhibiting strengths in problem solving, critical thinking, and decision making. The courses equipped me with the tools and insights on organizational management, labor laws, and community relations. Graduate school studies helped me hone my knowledge, skills, work experience, and leadership in the public sector by understanding government on every level as well as how they are shaped through public policy. Working for a municipality's political leadership, consequently working closely with senior executive administrators, fueled my desire to become a public administrator so I can lead the effective change in government. My current job aligns with what I thought I would be doing after college by working in the public sector, budgeting, and implementing new public policies/programs.

2. **What were some of the classes that really stood out to you in school that were influential in finding your career path?**

In undergrad, the course that set me on path of public administration was a local government course. I took the course in my final year and quarter of school as an easy class to pass with flying colors before graduation. While registering for the course I said to myself, "Who doesn't know government? This is going to be so easy." Little did I know, I knew nothing about Dayton's council manager form of government. Growing up in Columbus, Ohio, where the government structure was a strong mayor form, I was flabbergasted to learn other cities didn't follow my city's and other large cities' government structure. The course, taught by a former Dayton deputy city manager, directed my passion for civil service as I knew it through the lens of JROTC and not wanting to bear the responsibility of possibly becoming a combat soldier, to being a public administrator.

In graduate school, I really found that the organizational theory, public policy, and ethics in public administration courses influenced my enjoyment of working in government and my desire to earn my MPA. The ethics course especially spoke volumes to me in my aspiration of becoming a public administrator. At the time of my courses, I was working at a local municipality as an administrator for local political officials. During the coursework I began to realize how often public administrators and politicians are presented with ethical situations every day. I tend to believe more political officials than not straddle the line of being ethical and unethical, while public administrators tended to be steadfast on their ethical leadership for the betterment of the government and the citizens it serves. I found the class showed me the best way to address ethical situations personally and when it's presented to me as civil servant—even if your job is on the line from political pressure.

3. **What are some classes you wish you took now that you didn't take or didn't have the chance to take in college?**

I wish I would have taken more oral and writing-focused classes. The more and more you continue to grow in your field, the more you have to express your work, issues, and relay to the public what's going on in your organization. Verbal and written communication skills are key to climbing any organizational ladder. Other courses I wish I had the chance to take are courses on how government works with non profits and/or the public sector to leverage its resources to provide services or solutions to its citizens.

4. **What internships and/or co-curricular activities did you participate in and how did they prepare you for your graduate work and/or professional trajectory?**

I believe my continued work in local government coupled with my graduate course work provided tremendous individual growth and as civil servant. The course work provided me with the mental development that I needed to shore up the direction I wanted to go with my career in the public sector.

5. **What advice would you give to your undergraduate self? Or, in other words, what do you wish you knew as an undergraduate that you know now?**

I would tell my undergraduate self to explore why you enjoyed Air Force JROTC in high school while you're in college. You can still be involved in government even though you have concerns about your potential duties as combat soldier if you were to enlist. Being a public administrator will allow you to give back to your community and help those who are less fortunate like you were more than you could have ever done in the military. Your experience, resolve, and determination will allow you to be the change agent and affect public policy.

Jennifer Pautz is the director of government affairs for New York University. After earning an undergraduate degree in philosophy and political science at Elon University, she went on to earn both a Master of Public Administration and Juris Doctorate in a joint degree program at Syracuse University.

1. **What is your current job and how did your studies prepare you for this role? How does that job align with what you thought you'd be doing when you were in college?**

I currently serve as government affairs representative for higher education, specifically for NYU. I would not say that I imagined I would be in this role in college or that specifically studies in college prepared me for this exact role. I believe that the best lessons from college courses that I carry with me today are critical reading skills, the ability to absorb material and write quickly, and the ability to give presentations and speak publicly. While those skills can be applied to a multitude of fields, they are essential in government relations as I serve a generalist role where I must quickly understand complex problems in a variety of areas, strategize on how to solve them, and convince others to take action on them. Courses in graduate schools were more directly relevant to my field now in specifically analyzing legislation, laws, and regulations but I still would not say even in graduate school that I anticipated my current career path during my studies.

2. **What were some of the classes that really stood out to you in school that were influential in finding your career path?**

To be honest I would not say that any specific classes helped me find my career path; it was something that occurred after entering the workforce and understanding what kinds of opportunities really existed both in government and working with government from the outside. I certainly had classes that were engaging and interesting in subject matters that broadly relate to what I am doing now, but I would not characterize them as playing a role in determining a particular path.

3. **What are some classes you wish you took now that you didn't take or didn't have the chance to take in college?**

Looking back, I wish I spent more time in economics courses, public budgeting, and in courses focused on data management and utilization. While I had some requirements for both college and graduate school in statistics and basic data management, etc., they are such critical tools in the workforce today in every field that I wish I had more of a basis to build from. I did take economics and budgeting in graduate school but deeper dives would have been more helpful as everything in government revolves around budgeting. However, every level of government and state/municipality are different in their budget operations so it would be hard to teach budgeting courses that really prepare you for a specific role; it's just something you have to learn on the job.

4. **What internships and/or co-curricular activities did you participate in and how did they prepare you for your graduate work and/or professional trajectory?**

I had a series of internships in various areas of government including in the judicial system, public service law, executive branch and legislative branch positions. Those positions overall helped give me a frame of reference for how these offices work and what to expect when working with these offices. While I do not work for the government now, I would say that these experiences helped me learn how to work with government—and the people in government—in order to achieve my end goals. I also was involved in lot of co-curricular activities, especially in college, that perhaps taught me more about time management and prioritization as opposed to specific skills that related to my future career path. Those skills are critical, however, especially in government, which can tend to be reactionary and on a timeline.

5. **What advice would you give to your undergraduate self? Or, in other words, what do you wish you knew as an undergraduate that you know now?**

Besides skipping law school?! I actually talk a lot to undergraduates now so I think my advice would be what I tell them: don't feel pressured to know exactly what your career path will be and hold yourself to a rigid academic and/or professional timeline the day you graduate from college. Understanding the tools that public servants use on a daily basis (critical reading, quick absorption of issues and seeing how they connect, good—and quick—writing skills and being articulate) will allow you to move around in government, non profits, or as lobbyists, etc. easily. Over time you will have different jobs for different entities and all will help refine your skill set and knowledge base in particular policy areas. No one or two classes in college will specifically prepare you for any of it! Focus on learning the tools and then apply them in the workforce.

REFERENCES

Chapter 1

Curry, Kevin. 2017, April 6. American's public sector has a big problem—it's not getting any millennials. *The Hill*. Retrieved from http://thehill.com/blogs/pundits-blog/economy-budget/327638-americas-public-sector-has-a-big-problem-its-not-getting. Accessed 26 April 2018.

Goodsell, Charles T. 2015. *The new case for bureaucracy*. Washington, DC: CQ Press.

McKeever, Brice, and Marcus Gaddy. 2016, October 24. The nonprofit workforce: By the numbers. *Nonprofit Quarterly*. Retrieved from https://nonprofitquarterly.org/2016/10/24/nonprofit-workforce-numbers/. Accessed 3 May 2018.

Pautz, Michelle C. 2018. *Civil servants on the silver screen: Hollywood's depiction of government and bureaucrats*. Lanham, MD: Lexington.

Pew Research Center. 2017, December 14. Public trust in government: 1958-2017. Retrieved from http://www.people-press.org/2017/12/14/public-trust-in-government-1958-2017/. Accessed 26 April 2018.

U.S. Census Bureau. 2012. Census Bureau reports there are 89,004 local governments in the United States. Retrieved from https://www.census.gov/newsroom/releases/archives/governments/cb12-161.html. Accessed 3 May 2018.

U.S. Census Bureau. 2016, March. Annual survey of public employment and payroll. Retrieved from https://www.census.gov/programs-surveys/apes/newsroom/updates/2016-apes.html. Accessed 3 May 2018.

U.S. Office of Personnel Management. 2017. Profile of federal civilian non-postal employees. Available at https://www.opm.gov/policy-data-oversight/data-analysis-documentation/federal-employment-reports/reports-publications/profile-of-federal-civilian-non-postal-employees/. Accessed 3 May 2018.

Yoder, Eric. 2018, April 11. Federal employees lag behind private sector workers in salaries by 32 percent on average, report says. *The Washington Post*. Retrieved from https://www.washingtonpost.com/news/powerpost/wp/2018/04/11/federal-employees-lag-private-sector-workers-in-salaries-by-32-percent-on-average-report-says/?noredirect=on&utm_term=.773174a1cd95. Accessed 14 April 2018.

Chapter 2

Dweck, Carol S. 2007. *Mindset: The new psychology of success*. New York: Ballantine Books.

Chapter 3

The Devil Wears Prada. 2006. Twentieth Century Fox. Directed by David Frankel.

Schön, Donald A. 1984. *The reflective practitioner: How professionals think in action.* New York: Basic Books.

Chapter 4

Duckworth, Angela. 2016. *Grit: The power of passion and perseverance.* New York: Scribner.

Dweck, Carol S. 2007. *Mindset: The new psychology of success.* New York: Ballantine Books.

Perrin, Andrew. 2018, March 23. Who doesn't read books in America? *Pew Research Center.* Retrieved from http://www.pewresearch.org/fact-tank/2018/03/23/who-doesnt-read-books-in-america/. Accessed 17 July 2018.